A Special Gift

James and Deanna

George and Chandy

Christmas 2012

THE GLORY of CHRISTMAS

CHARLES SWINDOLL
MAX LUCADO
CHARLES COLSON

WORD PUBLISHING
Dallas • London • Vancouver • Melbourne

J. Countryman is a registered trademark of Word Publishing, Inc.
A J. Countryman Book

Designed by Koechel Peterson & Associates, Inc.
Minneapolis, Minnesota.

Compiled and edited by Terri Gibbs

Photographic Acknowledgments:
Bill Brooks/Masterfile, pages 41, 77, 120.
Ron Stroud/Masterfile, pages 19, 56, 61, 85, 94, 101, 119, 125.
Janet Foster/Masterfile, pages 7, 28, 82.
David Muir/Masterfile, pages 36, 46, 69.
Daryl Benson/Masterfile, pages 8, 15, 42, 52, 65, 102, 108, 113, 129, 140.
Jim Craigmyle/Masterfile, pages 3, 25, 89, 134.

ISBN: 0-8499-5273-5

Contents

The gift is not

from man to God.

It is from

God to man. . . .

Max Lucado

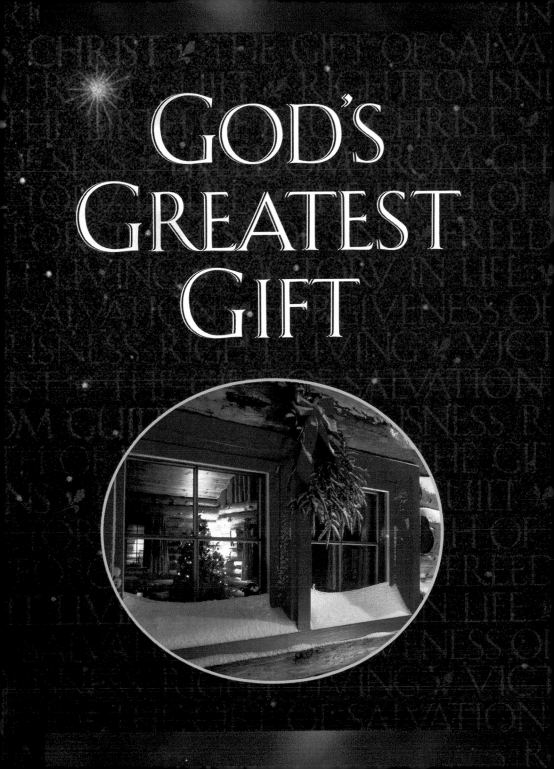

GOD'S GREATEST GIFT

THE BIRTH
of
JESUS CHRIST

hristmas comes each year to draw people in from the cold.

Like tiny frightened sparrows, shivering in the winter cold, many live their lives on the barren branches of heartbreak, disappointment, and loneliness, lost in thoughts of shame, self-pity, guilt, or failure. One blustery day follows another, and the only company they keep is with fellow-strugglers who land on the same branches, confused and unprotected.

We try so hard to attract them into the warmth. Week after week church bells ring. Choirs sing. Preachers preach. Lighted churches send out their beacon. But nothing seems to bring in those who need warmth the most.

Then, as the year draws to a close, Christmas offers its wonderful message. Emmanuel. God with us. He who resided in Heaven, co-equal and co-eternal with the Father and the Spirit, willingly descended into our world. He breathed our air, felt our pain, knew our sorrows, and died for our sins. He didn't come to frighten us, but to show us the way to warmth and safety.

CHARLES SWINDOLL
THE FINISHING TOUCH

HERE IS ONE WORD THAT DESCRIBES THE NIGHT HE CAME—ORDINARY.

that Jesus

The sky was ordinary. An occasional gust stirred the leaves and chilled the air. The stars were diamonds sparkling on black velvet. Fleets of clouds floated in front of the moon.

It was a beautiful night—a night worth peeking out your bedroom window to admire—but not really an unusual one. No reason to expect a surprise. Nothing to keep a person awake. An ordinary night with an ordinary sky.

The sheep were ordinary. Some fat. Some scrawny. Some with barrel bellies. Some with twig legs. Common animals. No fleece made of gold. No history makers. No blue-ribbon winners. They were simply sheep—lumpy, sleeping silhouettes on a hillside.

And the shepherds. Peasants they were. Probably wearing all the clothes they owned. Smelling like sheep and looking just as woolly. They were conscientious, willing to spend the night with their flocks. But you won't find their staffs in a museum nor their writings in a library. No one asked their opinion on social justice or the application of the Torah. They were nameless and simple.

(CONTINUED)

An ordinary night with ordinary sheep and ordinary shepherds.
And were it not for a God who loves to hook an "extra" on the front
of the ordinary, the night would have gone unnoticed. The sheep would
have been forgotten, and the shepherds would have slept the night away.

But God dances amidst the common. And that night he did a waltz.

The black sky exploded with brightness. Trees that had been
shadows jumped into clarity. Sheep that had been silent became a chorus
of curiosity. One minute the shepherd was dead asleep, the next he was
rubbing his eyes and staring into the face of an alien.

The night was ordinary no more.

The angel came in the night because that is when lights are best
seen and that is when they are most needed. God comes into the
common for the same reason.

place

HIS MOST POWERFUL
TOOLS ARE THE SIMPLEST.

MAX LUCADO
THE APPLAUSE OF HEAVEN

His ultimate weapon was the sacrifice of his own Son.

WHEN GOD WANTED TO DEFEAT SIN, his ultimate weapon was the sacrifice of his own Son. On Christmas Day two thousand years ago, the birth of a tiny baby in an obscure village in the Middle East was God's supreme triumph of good over evil.

CHARLES COLSON
A DANGEROUS GRACE

Untethered by time, [God] sees us all. From the backwoods of Virginia to the business district of London; from the Vikings to the astronauts, from the cave-dwellers to the kings, from the hut-builders to the finger-pointers to the rock-stackers, he sees us. Vagabonds and ragamuffins all, he saw us before we were born.

And he loves what he sees. Flooded by emotion. Overcome by pride, the Starmaker turns to us, one by one, and says, "You are my child. I love you dearly. I'm aware that someday you'll turn from me and walk away. But I want you to know, I've already provided a way back."

And to prove it, he did something extraordinary.

Stepping from the throne, he removed his robe of light and wrapped himself in skin: pigmented, human skin. The light of the universe entered a dark, wet womb. He whom angels worship nestled himself in the placenta of a peasant, was birthed into the cold night, and then slept on cow's hay.

Mary didn't know whether to give him milk or give him praise, but she gave him both since he was, as near as she could figure, hungry and holy.

Joseph didn't know whether to call him Junior or Father. But in the end called him Jesus, since that's what the angel had said and since he didn't have the faintest idea what to name a God he could cradle in his arms.

(CONTINUED)

... Don't you think ... their heads tilted and their minds wondered, "What in the world are you doing, God?" Or, better phrased, "God, what are you doing in the world?"

"Can anything make me stop loving you?" God asks. "Watch me speak your language, sleep on your earth, and feel your hurts. Behold the maker of sight and sound as he sneezes, coughs, and blows his nose. You wonder if I understand how you feel? Look into the dancing eyes of the kid in Nazareth; that's God walking to school. Ponder the toddler at Mary's table; that's God spilling his milk.

"You wonder how long my love will last? Find your answer on a splintered cross, on a craggy hill. That's me you see up there, your maker, your God, nail-stabbed and bleeding. Covered in spit and sin-soaked.

"THAT'S YOUR SIN I'M FEELING. THAT'S YOUR DEATH I'M DYING. THAT'S YOUR RESURRECTION I'M LIVING. THAT'S HOW MUCH I LOVE YOU."

MAX LUCADO
IN THE GRIP OF GRACE

THE GIFT
of
SALVATION

Rather than dismiss our sin, he assumes our sin...

WHAT A GOD!

Ponder the achievement of God.
He doesn't condone our sin, nor does he
compromise his standard.
He doesn't ignore our rebellion,
nor does he relax his demands.
Rather than dismiss our sin, he assumes
    our sin
and, incredibly, sentences himself.
God's holiness is honored. Our sin
    is punished . . .
and we are redeemed.
God does what we cannot do
so we can be what we dare not dream:
    perfect before God.

MAX LUCADO
IN THE GRIP OF GRACE

he conclusion is unavoidable: self–salvation simply does not work. Man has no way to save himself.

But Paul announces that God has a way. Where man fails God excels. Salvation comes from heaven downward, not earth upward. "A new day from heaven will dawn upon us" (Luke 1:78). "Every good action and every perfect gift is from God" (James 1:17).

Please note: Salvation is God–given, God–driven, God–empowered, and God–originated. The gift is not from man to God. It is from God to man.

Grace is created by God and given to man. . . . On the basis of this point alone, Christianity is set apart from any other religion in the world. . . . Every other approach to God is a bartering system; if I do this, God will do that. I'm either saved by works (what I do), emotions (what I experience), or knowledge (what I know).

By contrast, Christianity has no whiff of negotiation at all. Man is not the negotiator; indeed, man has no grounds from which to negotiate.

MAX LUCADO
IN THE GRIP OF GRACE

Imagine coming to a friend's house who has invited you over to enjoy a meal. You finish the delicious meal and then listen to some fine music and visit for a while. Finally, you stand up and get your coat as you prepare to leave. But before you leave you reach into your pocket and say, "Now, how much do I owe you?" What an insult! You don't do that with someone who has graciously given you a meal. Isn't it strange, though, how this world is running over with people who think there's something they must do to pay God back? Somehow they are hoping God will smile on them if they work real hard and earn his acceptance; but that's an acceptance on the basis of works. That's not the way it is with grace.

And now that Christ has come and died and thereby satisfied the Father's demands on sin, all we need to do is claim his grace by accepting the free gift of eternal life. Period.

HE SMILES ON US BECAUSE OF HIS SON'S DEATH AND RESURRECTION. IT'S GRACE, MY FRIEND, AMAZING GRACE.

CHARLES SWINDOLL
THE GRACE AWAKENING

FORGIVENESS _of_ SINS

he first step to joy is a plea for help, an acknowledgment of moral destitution, an admission of inward paucity. Those who taste God's presence have declared spiritual bankruptcy and are aware of their spiritual crisis. Their cupboards are bare. Their pockets are empty. Their options are gone. They have long since stopped demanding justice; they are pleading for mercy.

They don't brag; they beg.

They ask God to do for them what they can't do without him. They have seen how holy God is and how sinful they are and have agreed with Jesus' statement, "Salvation is impossible."

Oh, the irony of God's delight—born in the parched soil of destitution rather than the fertile ground of achievement.

It's a different path, a path we're not accustomed to taking. We don't often declare our impotence. Admission of failure is not usually admission into joy. Complete confession is not commonly followed by total pardon. But then again, God has never been governed by what is common.

MAX LUCADO
THE APPLAUSE OF HEAVEN

OR MOST OF US, the word *repentance* conjures up images of medieval monks in sackcloth or Old Testament prophets rending their garments in anguish. But repentance is much more than self-flagellation, more than regret, more than deep sorrow for past sins. The biblical word for repentance is *metanoia* in the Greek. *Meta* means "change" and noia means "mind," so literally it means "a change of mind."

Repentance is replete with radical implications, for a fundamental change of mind not only turns us from the sinful past, but also transforms our life plan, ethics, and actions as we begin to see the world through God's eyes rather than ours. That kind of transformation requires the ultimate surrender of self.

CHARLES COLSON
LOVING GOD

onfession does for the soul what preparing the land does for the field. Before the farmer sows the seed he works the acreage, removing the rocks and pulling the stumps. He knows that seed grows better if the land is prepared. Confession is the act of inviting God to walk the acreage of our hearts. "There is a rock of greed over here Father, I can't budge it. And that tree of guilt near the fence? Its roots are long and deep. And may I show you some dry soil, too crusty for seed?" God's seed grows better if the soil of the heart is cleared.

And so the Father and the Son walk the field together; digging and pulling, preparing the heart for fruit. Confession invites the Father to work the soil of the soul.

CONFESSION SEEKS PARDON FROM GOD, NOT AMNESTY.

MAX LUCADO
IN THE GRIP OF GRACE

Repentance is the process by which we see ourselves, day by day, as we really are: sinful, needy, dependent people. It is the process by which we see God as he is: awesome, majestic, and holy.

"The Christian needs the church to be a repenting community," proclaims Richard Neuhaus. "The Christian needs the church to be a zone of truth in a world of mendacity, to be a community in which our sin need not be disguised, but can be honestly faced and plainly confessed."

It was not by accident, I suspect, that the first of the ninety-five theses Martin Luther nailed to the Wittenberg church door read,

"WHEN OUR LORD AND MASTER JESUS CHRIST SAID 'REPENT,' HE WILLED THAT THE ENTIRE LIFE OF BELIEVERS BE ONE OF REPENTANCE."

CHARLES COLSON
AGAINST THE NIGHT

If you are in Christ . . . you are guaranteed that your sins will be filtered through, hidden in, and screened out by the sacrifice of Jesus. When God looks at you, he doesn't see you; he sees the One who surrounds you. That means that failure is not a concern for you. Your victory is secure. How could you not be courageous?

Picture it this way. Imagine that you are an ice skater in competition. You are in first place with one more round to go. If you perform well, the trophy is yours. You are nervous, anxious, and frightened.

Then, only minutes before your performance, your trainer rushes to you with the thrilling news: "You've already won! The judges tabulated the scores, and the person in second place can't catch you. You are too far ahead. "

Upon hearing that news, how will you feel? Exhilarated!

And how will you skate? Timidly? Cautiously? Of course not. How about courageously and confidently? You bet you will. You will do your best because the prize is yours. You will skate like a champion because that is what you are!

MAX LUCADO
THE APPLAUSE OF HEAVEN

FREEDOM
from
GUILT

God is
willing
to
forgive
all.

TO BELIEVE WE ARE TOTALLY AND ETERNALLY DEBT FREE IS SELDOM EASY. Even if we've stood before the throne and heard it from the king himself, we still doubt. As a result, many are forgiven only a little, not because the grace of the king is limited, but because the faith of the sinner is small. God is willing to forgive all. He's willing to wipe the slate completely clean. He guides us to a pool of mercy and invites us to bathe. Some plunge in, but others just touch the surface. They leave feeling unforgiven. . . .

Where the grace of God is missed, bitterness is born. But where the grace of God is embraced, forgiveness flourishes. . . .

The longer we walk in the garden, the more likely we are to smell like flowers. The more we immerse ourselves in grace, the more likely we are to give grace.

MAX LUCADO
IN THE GRIP OF GRACE

UMAITA, [A PRISON IN BRAZIL], HAS AN ASTONISHING RECORD. Its recidivism rate is 4 percent compared to 75 percent in the rest of Brazil and the United States. How is that possible?

I saw the answer when my inmate guide escorted me to the notorious punishment cell once used for torture. Today, he told me, that block houses only a single inmate. As we reached the end of the long concrete corridor and he put the key into the lock, he paused and asked, "Are you sure you want to go in?"

"Of course," I replied impatiently, "I've been in isolation cells all over the world." Slowly he swung open the massive door, and I saw the prisoner in that punishment cell: a crucifix, beautifully carved by the Humaita inmates—the Prisoner Jesus, hanging on the cross.

"He's doing time for all the rest of us," my guide said softly.

In that cross carved by loving hands is a holy subversion. It heralds change more radical than mankind's most fevered dreams. Its followers expand the boundaries of a Kingdom that can never fail. A shining Kingdom that reaches into the darkest corners of every community, into the darkest corners of every mind. A Kingdom of deathless hope, of restless virtue, of endless peace.

CHARLES COLSON
"ENDURING REVOLUTION"

RIGHTEOUSNESS:
Right Living

T'S QUIET. It's early. My coffee is hot. The sky is still black. The world is still asleep. The day is coming.

In a few moments the day will arrive. It will roar down the track with the rising of the sun. The stillness of the dawn will be exchanged for the noise of the day. The calm of solitude will be replaced by the pounding pace of the human race. The refuge of the early morning will be invaded by decisions to be made and deadlines to be met.

For the next twelve hours I will be exposed to the day's demands. It is now that I must make a choice. Because of Calvary, I'm free to choose. And so I choose.

I choose love . . .

No occasion justifies hatred; no injustice warrants bitterness. I choose love. Today I will love God and what God loves.

I choose joy . . .

I will invite my God to be the God of circumstance. I will refuse the temptation to be cynical . . . the tool of the lazy thinker. I will refuse to see people as anything less than human beings, created by God. I will refuse to see any problem as anything less than an opportunity to see God.

(CONTINUED)

I choose peace . . .

I will live forgiven. I will forgive so that I may live.

I choose patience . . .

I will overlook the inconveniences of the world. Instead of cursing the one who takes my place, I'll invite him to do so. Rather than complain that the wait is too long, I will thank God for a moment to pray. Instead of clinching my fist at new assignments, I will face them with joy and courage.

I choose kindness . . .

I will be kind to the poor, for they are alone. Kind to the rich, for they are afraid. And kind to the unkind, for such is how God has treated me.

I choose goodness . . .

I will go without a dollar before I take a dishonest one. I will be overlooked before I will boast. I will confess before I will accuse. I choose goodness.

(CONTINUED)

I choose faithfulness . . .

Today I will keep my promises. My debtors will not regret their trust. My associates will not question my word. My wife will not question my love. And my children will never fear that their father will not come home.

I choose gentleness . . .

Nothing is won by force. I choose to be gentle. If I raise my voice may it be only in praise. If I clench my fist, may it be only in prayer. If I make a demand, may it be only of myself.

I choose self-control . . .

I am a spiritual being. After this body is dead, my spirit will soar. I refuse to let what will rot, rule the eternal. I choose self-control. I will be drunk only by joy. I will be impassioned only by my faith. I will be influenced only by God. I will be taught only by Christ. I choose self-control.

Love, joy, peace, patience, kindness, goodness, faithfulness, gentleness, and self-control. To these I commit my day. If I succeed, I will give thanks. If I fail, I will seek his grace. And then, when this day is done, I will place my head on my pillow and rest.

MAX LUCADO
WHEN GOD WHISPERS YOUR NAME

Stop and think: Upon believing in Jesus Christ's substitutionary death and bodily resurrection, the once-lost sinner is instantly, unconditionally, and permanently "declared 100% righteous." Anything less and we are not righteous . . . we're *almost* righteous.

If we were declared 99.9% righteous, some verses would have to be rewritten. Like Isaiah 1:18, which might then read: "'Come now, and let us reason together,' says the Lord, 'Though your sins are as scarlet, they will be light pink.'"

Nonsense! The promise of sins forgiven is all or nothing. Eighty percent won't cut it . . . or 90% . . . or 99 and 44/100% . . . or 99.9%. Let's face it, 0.1% is still sinful. I mean, would you drink a gallon of water with only one tiny drop of strychnine in it? Would you feel comfortable having a surgeon cut on you who was wearing almost-sterile gloves?

WHEN OUR LORD SAID "IT IS FINISHED," HE MEANT "FINISHED." THE COLOSSAL RANSOM FOR SIN WAS FULLY PAID. HE SATISFIED THE FATHER'S DEMAND.

CHARLES SWINDOLL
THE FINISHING TOUCH

We should never deify any person, idea, or political system.

MANY PEOPLE ASSUME THAT ANYONE WHO HOLDS ABSOLUTE MORAL PRINCIPLES MUST AUTOMATICALLY BE ABSOLUTIST IN MENTALITY AS WELL: RIGID, INFLEXIBLE, AND HOSTILE. BUT THERE ARE TWO COMPLETELY DIFFERENT KINDS OF ABSOLUTES.

For Christians, God himself is the only absolute; truth and ethics are rooted in his character. This keeps us from looking for absolutes anywhere in the created world. We should never deify any person, idea, or political system.

Secular absolutes are often advanced by the power of the sword. But transcendent absolutes, when rightly understood, foster tolerance—because our ultimate allegiance is to the things above, not to any group or government deified here on earth.

CHARLES COLSON
A DANCE WITH DECEPTION

Before Christ our lives were out of control...

HOW COULD WE WHO HAVE BEEN FREED FROM SIN RETURN TO IT? Before Christ our lives were out of control, sloppy, and indulgent. We didn't even know we were slobs until we met him.

Then he moved in. Things began to change. What we threw around we began putting away. What we neglected we cleaned up. What had been clutter became order. Oh, there were and still are occasional lapses of thought and deed, but by and large he got our house in order.

Suddenly we find ourselves wanting to do good. Go back to the old mess? Are you kidding? "In the past you were slaves to sin—sin controlled you. But thank God, you fully obeyed the things that you were taught. You were made free from sin, and now you are slaves to goodness" (Rom. 6: 17–18).

MAX LUCADO
IN THE GRIP OF GRACE

HROUGHOUT HIS PUBLIC MINISTRY, JESUS EVOKED THE KINGDOM MIND-SET THAT CONSCIOUSLY TAKES "EVERY THOUGHT CAPTIVE TO THE OBEDIENCE OF CHRIST" (2 COR. 10:5, NASB). Likening the kingdom of heaven to leaven, Jesus described God's rule as having a transforming effect on everything it touches. And in the parable of the talents he taught that God expects a "return on investments" from his faithful stewards, who are to bring glory to him as they cultivate and keep that which he has entrusted to them.

The apostles took pains to teach the church not to be conformed to this world but to be transformed by the renewing of the mind, to guard against being taken captive by the empty deceptions and philosophies of the world or cleverly devised tales, and to seek truth according to Christ.

From creation onward, God's rule extends to everything. From our bank accounts to our business dealings to our educational curriculum to social justice issues to environmental concerns to our political choices—everything must reflect the fact that God's righteous rule extends to all of life.

CHARLES COLSON
THE BODY

VICTORY
in
LIFE

NE EASTER MORNING, AS I SAT IN THE CHAPEL AT THE DELAWARE STATE PRISON WAITING TO PREACH, MY MIND DRIFTED BACK IN TIME . . . to scholarships and honors earned, cases argued and won, great decisions made from lofty government offices. My life had been the perfect success story, the great American dream fulfilled.

But all at once I realized that it was not my success God had used to enable me to help those in this prison, or in hundreds others like it. My life of success was not what made this morning so glorious—all my achievements meant nothing in God's economy. No, the real legacy of my life was my biggest failure—that I was an ex-convict. My greatest humiliation—being sent to prison—was the beginning of God's greatest use of my life; he chose the one experience in which I could not glory for *his* glory.

Confronted with this staggering truth, I understood with a jolt that I had been looking at life backward. But now I could see: Only when I lost everything that I thought made Charles Colson a great guy had I found the true self God intended me to be and the true purpose of my life.

It is not what we do that matters, *but what a sovereign God chooses to do through us.*

CHARLES COLSON
LOVING GOD

T IS GOD'S GLADNESS. IT'S SACRED DELIGHT.

And it is this sacred delight that Jesus promises in the Sermon on the Mount. . . .

But this joy is not cheap. What Jesus promises is not a gimmick to give you goose bumps nor a mental attitude that has to be pumped up at pep rallies. No, Matthew 5 describes God's radical reconstruction of the heart.

Observe the sequence. First, we recognize we are in need (we're poor in spirit). Next, we repent of our self–sufficiency (we mourn). We quit calling the shots and surrender control to God (we're meek). So grateful are we for his presence that we yearn for more of him (we hunger and thirst). As we grow closer to him, we become more like him. We forgive others (we're merciful). We change our outlook (we're pure in heart). We love others (we're peace–makers). We endure injustice (we're persecuted).

It's no casual shift of attitude. It is a demolition of the old structure and a creation of the new. The more radical the change, the greater the joy. And it's worth every effort, for this is the joy of God.

MAX LUCADO
THE APPLAUSE OF HEAVEN

 n *The Christian Mind*, Harry Blamires says the typical believer prays sincerely about his work but never talks candidly with his non-Christian colleagues about his faith. He is only comfortable evaluating his spiritual life in a "spiritual" context. This results in spiritual schizophrenia as the Christian bounces back and forth between the stock market and sanctification.

Such categorizing would be plausible if Christianity were nothing more than a moral code, an AA pledge, or a self-help course. But Christianity claims to be the central fact of human history: the God who created man invaded the world in the person of Jesus Christ, died, was resurrected, ascended, and lives today, sovereign over all.

If this claim is valid—if Christianity is true—then it cannot be simply a file drawer in our crowded lives. It must be the central truth from which all our behavior, relationships, and philosophy flow. We must set all earthly issues within the context of the eternal.

CHARLES COLSON
AGAINST THE NIGHT

The kingdom of
God embraces every
aspect of life: ethical,
spiritual, and temporal.

Charles Colson

FRIENDSHIP
WITH GOD

ADOPTED CHILDREN
of the
KING

 othing distinguishes the kingdoms of man from the kingdom of God more than their diametrically opposed views of the exercise of power. One seeks to control people, the other to serve people; one promotes self, the other prostrates self; one seeks prestige and position, the other lifts up the lowly and despised. As citizens of the Kingdom today practice this view of power, they are setting an example for their neighbors by modeling servanthood.

This does not mean that the Christian can't use power. In positions of leadership, especially in government institutions to which God has specifically granted the power of the sword, the Christian can do so in good conscience. But the Christian uses power with a different motive and in different ways: not to impose his or her personal will over others but to preserve God's plan for order and justice for all.

CHARLES COLSON
KINGDOMS IN CONFLICT

As youngsters, we neighborhood kids would play street football. The minute we got home from school, we'd drop the books and hit the pavement. The kid across the street had a dad with a great arm and a strong addiction to football. As soon as he'd pull in the driveway from work we'd start yelling for him to come and play ball. He couldn't resist. Out of fairness he'd always ask, "Which team is losing?" Then he would join that team, which often seemed to be mine.

His appearance in the huddle changed the whole ball game. He was confident, strong, and most of all, he had a plan. We'd circle around him, and he'd look at us and say, "OK boys, here is what we are going to do." The other side was groaning before we left the huddle. You see, we not only had a new plan, we had a new leader.

HE BROUGHT NEW LIFE TO OUR TEAM. GOD DOES PRECISELY THE SAME. WE DIDN'T NEED A NEW PLAY; WE NEEDED A NEW PLAN. WE DIDN'T NEED TO TRADE POSITIONS; WE NEEDED A NEW PLAYER. THAT PLAYER IS JESUS CHRIST, GOD'S FIRSTBORN SON.

MAX LUCADO
IN THE GRIP OF GRACE

hristianity is more than simply a relationship between man and God. The kingdom of God embraces every aspect of life: ethical, spiritual, and temporal.

In announcing an all-encompassing Kingdom, Jesus was not using a clever metaphor; he was expressing the literal theme of Jewish history—that God was King and the people were his subjects. This tradition dated back to the days of Abraham and the patriarchs, when God made his original covenant with the Jews to be his "holy nation."

David, the first great king of the Jews, consolidated a visible kingdom for the people of God. But it was to be only a reflection of the ultimate rule of God, their true King. Later, when the Jews were conquered and sent into exile, the prophets promised the coming of Messiah and the eventual establishment of the kingdom of God. Christ was the fulfillment of that prophecy; he was the final king in David's royal line.

But Jesus was not just a king for Israel; he was King for all people.

CHARLES COLSON
KINGDOMS IN CONFLICT

OUR COMFORT AND POWER, *the* HOLY SPIRIT

PIRITUAL LIFE COMES FROM THE
SPIRIT! YOUR PARENTS MAY HAVE
GIVEN YOU GENES, BUT GOD GIVES
YOU GRACE. Your parents may be
responsible for your body, but God has taken
charge of your soul. You may get your looks from your mother,
but you get eternity from your Father, your heavenly Father. . . .

God has not left you adrift on a sea of heredity. . . . You
cannot control the way your forefathers responded to God. But
you can control the way you respond to him. The past does not
have to be your prison. You have a voice in your destiny. You
have a say in your life. You have a choice in the path you take.

Choose well and someday—generations from now—your
grandchildren and great-grandchildren will thank God for the
seeds you sowed.

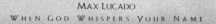

MAX LUCADO
WHEN GOD WHISPERS YOUR NAME

He energizes us to stay the course.

WE BECOME CHRISTIANS
BECAUSE WE "RECEIVED
CHRIST JESUS THE LORD."
We become empowered and filled with
the Spirit as we "walk in him."

What fuel is to a car, the Holy
Spirit is to the believer. He energizes
us to stay the course. He motivates us
in spite of the obstacles. He keeps us
going when the road gets rough. It is
the Spirit who comforts us in our
distress, who calms us in times of
calamity, who becomes our companion
in loneliness and grief, who spurs our
"intuition" into action, who fills our
minds with discernment when we are
uneasy about a certain decision. In
short, he is our spiritual fuel. When we
attempt to operate without him or to
use some substitute fuel, all systems
grind to a halt.

CHARLES SWINDOLL
FLYING CLOSER TO THE FLAME

t some point we need more than good advice; we need help. Somewhere on this journey home we realize that a fifty–fifty proposition is too little. We need more . . .

We need help. Help from the inside out. The kind of help Jesus promised. "I will ask the Father, and he will give you another Helper to be with you forever—the Spirit of truth. The world cannot accept him, because it does not see him or know him. But you know him because he lives with you and will be *in* you" (John 14:16–17, emphasis mine).

Note the final words of the verse. And in doing so, note the dwelling place of God—"in you." Not near us. Not above us. Not around us. But in us. In the part of us we don't even know. In the heart no one else has seen. In the hidden recesses of our being dwells, not an angel, not a philosophy, not a genie, but God. Imagine that.

MAX LUCADO
WHEN GOD WHISPERS YOUR NAME

Thoughts are the thermostat that regulates what we accomplish in life. My body responds and reacts to the input from my mind. If I feed my mind upon doubt, disbelief, and discouragement, that is precisely the kind of day my body will experience. If I adjust my thermostat forward to thoughts filled with vision, vitality, and victory, I can count on that kind of day. Thus, you and I become what we think about. . . .

Thoughts, positive or negative, grow stronger when fertilized with constant repetition. That may explain why so many who are gloomy and gray stay in that mood . . . and why those who are cheery and enthusiastic continue to be so. . . .

You need only one foreman in your mental factory: Mr. Triumph is his name. He is anxious to assist you and available to all the members of God's family.

HIS REAL NAME IS THE HOLY SPIRIT, THE HELPER.

CHARLES SWINDOLL
THE FINISHING TOUCH

The Holy Spirit is the presence of God in our lives...

"THE TRUE CHILDREN OF GOD ARE THOSE WHO LET GOD'S SPIRIT LEAD THEM" (ROM. 8:14).

To hear many of us talk, you'd think we didn't believe these verses. You'd think we didn't believe in the Trinity. We talk about the Father and study the Son—but when it comes to the Holy Spirit, we are confused at best and frightened at worst. Confused because we've never been taught. Frightened because we've been taught to be afraid.

May I simplify things a bit? The Holy Spirit is the presence of God in our lives, carrying on the work of Jesus. The Holy Spirit helps us in three directions—inwardly (by granting us the fruits of the Spirit, Gal. 5:22–24), upwardly (by praying for us, Rom. 8:26) and outwardly (by pouring God's love into our hearts, Rom. 5:5).

MAX LUCADO
WHEN GOD WHISPERS YOUR NAME

THE
ASSURANCE
of
GOD'S LOVE

HERE IS NO WAY OUR LITTLE MINDS CAN COMPREHEND THE LOVE OF GOD. BUT THAT DIDN'T KEEP HIM FROM COMING....

From the cradle in Bethlehem to the cross in Jerusalem we've pondered the love of our Father. What can you say to that kind of emotion? Upon learning that God would rather die than live without you, how do you react? How can you begin to explain such passion?

MAX LUCADO
IN THE GRIP OF GRACE

From a distance, we dazzle; up close, we're tarnished. Put enough of us together and we may resemble an impressive mountain range. But when you get down into the shadowy crevices . . . the Alps we ain't.

That's why our Lord means so much to us. He is intimately acquainted with all our ways. Darkness and light are alike to him. Not one of us is hidden from his sight. All things are open and laid bare before him: our darkest secret, our deepest shame, our stormy past, our worst thought, our hidden motive, our vilest imagination . . . even our vain attempts to cover the ugly with snow-white beauty.

He comes up so close. He sees it all. He knows our frame. He remembers we are dust.

BEST OF ALL, HE LOVES US STILL.

CHARLES SWINDOLL
THE FINISHING TOUCH

here are many reasons God saves you: to bring glory to himself, to appease his justice, to demonstrate his sovereignty. But one of the sweetest reasons God saved you is because he is fond of you. He likes having you around. He thinks you are the best thing to come down the pike in quite awhile. . .

If God had a refrigerator, your picture would be on it. If he had a wallet, your photo would be in it. He sends you flowers every spring and a sunrise every morning. Whenever you want to talk, he'll listen. He can live anywhere in the universe, and he chose your heart. And the Christmas gift he sent you in Bethlehem?

FACE IT, FRIEND.
HE'S CRAZY ABOUT YOU.

MAX LUCADO
A GENTLE THUNDER

GOD
Is Our
REFUGE

God is for you.

"IF GOD IS FOR US, WHO CAN BE AGAINST US?" (ROM. 8:31 NIV).

The question is not simply, "Who can be against us?" You could answer that one. Who is against you? Disease, inflation, corruption, exhaustion. Calamities confront, and fears imprison. Were Paul's question, "Who can be against us?" we could list our foes much easier than we could fight them. But that is not the question. The question is, *If GOD IS FOR US, who can be against us?*

God is for you. Your parents may have forgotten you, your teachers may have neglected you, your siblings may be ashamed of you; but within reach of your prayers is the maker of the oceans. God! . . .

MAX LUCADO
IN THE GRIP OF GRACE

he remarkable promise that God made to Moses—that he would pitch his tent and dwell in the midst of his people—is a central theme throughout Scripture. In the familiar passage of John 1, "The Word became flesh, and *dwelt* among us," the Greek word for *dwelt* literally means to "pitch a tent." Through Christ, God comes to "pitch his tent" among his people. . . .

From Exodus to Revelation we find the identical imagery: a holy God "pitching his tent" among his people. First in the tabernacle, then in Christ, and ultimately in his kingdom. By pitching his tent in our midst, God identified with his people through his very presence. The reality of a "God who is here"—personal and in our midst—is an extraordinary assurance, one that distinguishes the Judeo-Christian faith from all other religions.

CHARLES COLSON
LOVING GOD

...he is waiting in the midst of the storm.

AS LONG AS JESUS IS ONE OF MANY OPTIONS, HE IS NO OPTION.

As long as you can carry your burdens alone, you don't need a burden bearer. As long as your situation brings you no grief, you will receive no comfort. And as long as you can take him or leave him, you might as well leave him, because he won't be taken half-heartedly

But when you mourn, when you get to the point of sorrow for your sins, when you admit that you have no other option but to cast all your cares on him, and when there is truly no other name that you can call, then cast all your cares on him, for he is waiting in the midst of the storm.

MAX LUCADO
THE APPLAUSE OF HEAVEN

In our world of superficial talk and casual relationships, it is easy to forget that a smile doesn't necessarily mean "I'm happy" and the courteous answer "I'm fine" may not be at all truthful. . . .

I'm not suggesting that everyone is an emotional time bomb or that masks are worn by all who seem to be enjoying life. But I've lived long enough to know that many a heart hides agony while the face reflects ecstasy.

There is Someone, however, who fully knows what lurks in our hearts. And knowing, he never laughs mockingly and fades away. He never shrugs and walks away. Instead, he understands completely and stays near.

Who, indeed, knows? Our God, alone, knows. He sympathizes with our weaknesses and forgives all our transgressions. To him there are no secret struggles or silent cries.

HE HEARS. HE SEES. HE STAYS NEAR.
HE ACCEPTS US AND LOVES US
UNCONDITIONALLY. HE IS "THE FATHER OF
MERCIES AND THE GOD OF ALL COMFORT."

CHARLES SWINDOLL
THE FINISHING TOUCH

AN UNFAILING
Friend

od is *for* you. Turn to the sidelines; that's God cheering your run. Look past the finish line; that's God applauding your steps. Listen for him in the bleachers, shouting your name. Too tired to continue? He'll carry you. Too discouraged to fight? He's picking you up. God is for you.

God is for *you*. Had he a calendar, your birthday would be circled. If he drove a car, your name would be on his bumper. If there's a tree in heaven, he's carved your name in the bark. . . .

"Can a mother forget the baby at her breast and have no compassion on the child she has borne?" God asks in Isaiah 49:15 (NIV). What a bizarre question. Can you mothers imagine feeding your infant and then later asking, "What was that baby's name?" No. I've seen you care for your young. You stroke the hair, you touch the face, you sing the name over and over. Can a mother forget? No way. But "even if she could forget, . . . I will not forget you," God pledges (Isa. 49:15).

MAX LUCADO
IN THE GRIP OF GRACE

. . . take

up his

cross

and

follow.

"JESUS IS LORD." THIS CONFESSION IS ONE OF THE OLDEST CHRISTIAN CREEDS. . . .

The Scriptures make clear the totality of Christ's claims upon us: "If anyone would come after me, he must deny himself and take up his cross and follow" (Matt. 16:24). . . .

If we really understand what being Christian means—that this Christ, the living God, actually comes in to rule one's life—then everything must change: Values, goals, desires, habits. If Christ's lordship does not disrupt our own lordship, then we must question the reality of our conversion.

CHARLES COLSON
WHO SPEAKS FOR GOD?

od's Book is a veritable storehouse of promises—over seven thousand of them. Not empty hopes and dreams, not just nice-sounding, eloquently worded thoughts that make you feel warm all over, but promises. Verbal guarantees in writing, signed by the Creator himself, in which he declares he will do or will refrain from doing specific things.

In a world of liars, cheats, deceivers, and con artists, isn't it a relief to know there is Someone you can trust? If he said it, you can count on it. Unlike the rhetoric of politicians who promise anybody anything they want to hear to get elected, what God says, God does.

CHARLES SWINDOLL
THE FINISHING TOUCH

GOD'S
COMPASSION
and
CARE

Storm clouds gather. Problem is, they're the wrong kind. We need rain desperately, but these clouds hold no rain. We need refreshment and renewal, a kind of inner relief. Like you feel when a sudden cloud cover blocks the burning rays of the sun and blows a cool breeze across the back of your neck. But the storm clouds I refer to bring no such relief. . . .

Storm clouds without rain. War clouds without relief . . . such clouds not only cast ominous shadows of uneasiness, they breed pessimism. . . .

Lest you forget, [God] is still in charge. As the prophet Nahum stated so confidently: "The Lord is slow to anger and great in power; the Lord will not leave the guilty unpunished. His way is in the whirlwind and the storm, and clouds are the dust of his feet" (Nah. 1:3 NIV). . . .

WHEN GOD IS IN CLEAR FOCUS,
HIS POWERFUL PRESENCE ECLIPSES OUR FEARS.
THE CLOUDS BECOME NOTHING MORE THAN
"THE DUST OF HIS FEET."

CHARLES SWINDOLL
THE FINISHING TOUCH

till we worry. We worry about the IRS and the SAT and the FBI. We worry about education, recreation, and constipation. We worry that we won't have enough money, and when we have money we worry that we won't manage it well. We worry that the world will end before the parking meter expires. We worry what the dog thinks if he sees us step out of the shower. We worry that someday we'll learn that fat-free yogurt was fattening.

Honestly, now. Did God save you so you would fret? Would he teach you to walk just to watch you fall? Would he be nailed to the cross for your sins and then disregard your prayers? Come on. Is Scripture teasing us when it reads, "He has put his angels in charge of you to watch over you wherever you go"? (Ps. 91:11).

I don't think so either.

When his joy

invades our lives,

it spills over into everything

we do and onto everyone we touch.

Charles Swindoll

LIVING
BEYOND
BELIEF

TRANSFORMED *into* GODLINESS

odliness is something below the surface of a life, deep down in the realm of attitude . . . an attitude toward God himself.

The longer I think about this, the more I believe that a person who is godly is one whose heart is sensitive toward God, one who takes God seriously. This evidences itself in one very obvious mannerism: the godly individual hungers and thirsts after God. In the words of the psalmist, the godly person has a soul that "pants" for the living god (Ps. 42:1–2).

Godly people possess an attitude of willing submission to God's will and ways. Whatever he says goes. And whatever it takes to carry it out is the very thing the godly desire to do.

CHARLES SWINDOLL
THE FINISHING TOUCH

Christianity doesn't make people perfect. But it does make us better than we would have been without it. Remove the restraint of God's law, and the worst barbarism breaks forth.

C. S. Lewis put it this way. A crotchety old lady may be considered a poor witness for Christian faith. But who is to say how much *more* cantankerous she might be if she were not a Christian? And a nonbeliever who is a gentle, pleasant fellow—who is to say how much better he might be if he *were* a Christian? . . .

DESPITE OUR HUMAN FAULTS, CHRISTIANITY HAS MADE THE WORLD AND THE PEOPLE IN IT—NOT PERFECT—BUT FAR BETTER THAN THEY WOULD HAVE BEEN WITHOUT IT.

CHARLES COLSON
A DANCE WITH DECEPTION

YOU WANT TO MAKE A
DIFFERENCE IN YOUR WORLD?
LIVE A HOLY LIFE:

Be faithful to your spouse.

Be the one at the office who
refuses to cheat.

Be the neighbor who acts neighborly.

Be the employee who does the work
and doesn't complain.

Pay your bills.

Do your part and enjoy life.

Don't speak one message and
live another.

People are watching the way we
act more than they are listening to
what we say.

MAX LUCADO
A GENTLE THUNDER

NYONE WHO LOVES THE SEA HAS A ROMANCE WITH IT AS WELL AS A RESPECT FOR IT. The romance is difficult to describe except by poets—for it defies analysis. The mind moves into another gear as the primeval rhythms of the seashore erode tidy resolutions and hectic deadlines. Time tables, appointments, and schedules are blurred by the salt mist. The thundering waves pull us with a powerful magnetism we cannot resist as we toss our cares and responsibilities to the prevailing winds. . . .

What is hidden in the sea is also hidden in God's wisdom. . . .

Those fathomless truths about him and those profound insights from him produce within us a wisdom that enables us to think with him. Such wisdom comes from his Spirit who, alone, can plumb the depths and reveal his mind.

The hurried, the greedy, the impatient cannot enter into such mysteries. God grants such understanding only to those who wait in silence . . . who respect "the depths of God." It takes time. It calls for solitude.

CHARLES SWINDOLL
THE FINISHING TOUCH

t is in the heart that most conversions begin. The baby believer's blissful world is filled with exciting new experiences: love of a kind not known before, forgiveness, inner peace. Emotions of the heart.

So it is understandable that sins of the heart, such as temper, hatred, jealousy, and pride, are the first to be affected in one's conversion. But that is only the beginning, only one part of the transforming process God intends for our lives. If we are to be new creations, much more is demanded: heart, body, spirit, *and* mind. . . .

This leap from the sin of this world to the holiness of the next is breathtaking even to contemplate.

Yet . . . the Christian *must* make a break with the past so radical that his mind is filled with the thoughts of Christ himself.

CHARLES COLSON
LIFE SENTENCE

ONTENT. THAT'S THE WORD. A STATE OF HEART IN WHICH YOU WOULD BE AT PEACE IF GOD GAVE YOU NOTHING MORE THAN HE ALREADY HAS. Test this question: What if God's only gift to you were his grace to save you. Would you be content? You beg him to save the life of your child. You plead with him to keep your business afloat. You implore him to remove the cancer from your body. What if his answer is, "My grace is enough." Would you be content?

You see, from heaven's perspective, grace is enough. If God did nothing more than save us from hell, could anyone complain? . . . Having been given eternal life, dare we grumble at an aching body? Having been given heavenly riches, dare we bemoan earthly poverty?

Let me be quick to add, God has not left you with "just salvation." If you have eyes to read these words, hands to hold this book, the means to own this volume, he has already given you grace upon grace. The vast majority of us have been saved and then blessed even more!

MAX LUCADO
IN THE GRIP OF GRACE

A Life
of
Fulfillment

During a visit to Australia, I was interviewed by a well–known radio host. As the program drew to a close, he posed one last question. "Mr. Colson, you are an unusual person. You have conquered the pinnacles of secular success. The goals most people strive their whole lives for, you have achieved—only to see it all collapse as you fell from the White House to prison. But now you're out, leading a new life as a Christian. It's like having lived two lives. How would you sum up the meaning of those two lives?"

I glanced at the clock. Only twenty seconds remained in the live broadcast. Then in a flash the "short" answer came. "If my life stands for anything," I said quickly, "it is the truth of the teaching of Jesus Christ, '. . . whoever wants to save his life will lose it, but whoever loses his life for me will find it. What good will it be for a man if he gains the whole world, yet forfeits his soul?'" (Matt. 16:25–26).

I had spent my first forty years seeking the whole world, to the neglect of my soul. But what I couldn't find in my quest for power and success—true security and meaning—I discovered in prison where all worldly props had been stripped away.

AND BY GOD'S GRACE, I LOST MY LIFE THAT I MIGHT FIND TRUE LIFE IN CHRIST.

CHARLES COLSON
WHO SPEAKS FOR GOD?

E ARE A SUCCESS-SATURATED SOCIETY. The tell-tale signs are everywhere. Each year dozens of books and magazines, scores of audio and video tapes, and hundreds of seminars offer ideas, motivation, techniques, and promises of prosperity.

Curiously, however, few ever address what it is most folks want (but seldom find) in their pursuit of success: contentment, fulfillment, satisfaction, and relief. On the contrary, the roads that are supposed to lead to success are not only rocky, they're maddening. . . .

At the risk of sounding ultra-simplistic, I'd like to offer some counsel that stands 180 degrees in contrast to all the above.

First, submit yourself to those who are wise. . . .

Second, humble yourself under God's mighty hand. . . .

Third, throw yourself on the mercy and care of God. . . .

CHARLES SWINDOLL
THE FINISHING TOUCH

Here is what we want to know. We want to know how long God's love will endure. . . . Does God really love us forever? Not just on Easter Sunday when our shoes are shined and our hair is fixed. We want to know . . . how does God feel about me when I'm a jerk? Not when I'm peppy and positive and ready to tackle world hunger. Not then. I know how he feels about me then. Even I like me then.

I want to know how he feels about me when I snap at anything that moves, when my thoughts are gutter-level, when my tongue is sharp enough to slice a rock. How does he feel about me then? . . .

Can anything separate us from the love Christ has for us?

God answered our question before we asked it. So we'd see his answer, he lit the sky with a star. So we'd hear it, he filled the night with a choir; and so we'd believe it, he did what no man had ever dreamed. He became flesh and dwelt among us.

HE PLACED HIS HAND ON THE SHOULDER OF HUMANITY AND SAID, "YOU'RE SOMETHING SPECIAL."

MAX LUCADO
IN THE GRIP OF GRACE

 piano sits in a room, gathering dust. It is full of the music of the masters, but in order for such strains to flow from it, fingers must strike the keys . . . trained fingers, representing endless hours of disciplined dedication. You do not have to practice. The piano neither requires it nor demands it. If, however, you want to draw beautiful music from the piano, that discipline is required. . . .

You do not have to pay the price to grow and expand intellectually. The mind neither requires it nor demands it. If, however, you want to experience the joy of discovery and the pleasure of plowing new and fertile soil, effort is required.

Light won't automatically shine upon you nor will truth silently seep into your head by means of rocking-chair osmosis.

It's up to you. It's your move.

CHARLES SWINDOLL
THE FINISHING TOUCH

HAPPINESS *in* CHRIST

NE BRISK DECEMBER NIGHT as I accompanied the president from the Oval Office in the West Wing of the White House, to the Residence, Mr. Nixon was musing about what people wanted in their leaders. He slowed a moment, looking into the distance across the South Lawn, and said, "The people really want a leader a little bigger than themselves, don't they, Charles? There's a certain aloofness, a power that's exuded by great men that people feel and want to follow."

But Jesus Christ exhibited none of this self-conscious aloofness. He served others first; he spoke to those to whom no one spoke; he dined with the lowest members of society; he touched the untouchables; he washed his servants' feet. He had no throne, no crown, no bevy of servants or armored guards. A borrowed manger and a borrowed tomb framed his earthly life.

Kings and presidents and prime ministers surround themselves with minions who rush ahead, swing the doors wide, and stand at attention as they wait for the great to pass. Jesus said that he himself stands at the door and knocks, patiently waiting to enter our lives.

CHARLES COLSON
KINGDOMS IN CONFLICT

Back when I was in grade school, it was always a special treat when the teacher gave the class permission to do something unusual.

I remember one hot and humid Houston afternoon when she gave everyone permission to go barefoot after lunch. We got to pull off our socks, stick 'em in our sneakers, and wiggle our toes all we wanted to. During the afternoon recess that extra freedom added great speed to our softball game on the playground. . . .

Isn't it strange then, now that you and I are grown and have become Christians, how reluctant we are to give ourselves permission to do . . . to think . . . to say . . . to buy and enjoy . . . or to be different and not worry about who may say what?

EVEN THOUGH OUR GOD HAS GRACIOUSLY GRANTED US PERMISSION TO BE FREE, TO HAVE LIBERTY, TO BREAK THE CHAINS OF RIGIDITY, AND TO ENJOY SO MUCH OF THIS LIFE, MANY IN HIS FAMILY SELDOM GIVE THEMSELVES PERMISSION.

CHARLES SWINDOLL
THE FINISHING TOUCH

THE TRUE
MEANING
of
PEACE

Somewhere, miles away, crops push their way toward harvest and waves roar and tumble onto shore. Windswept forests sing their timeless songs, and desert animals scurry in the shadows of cactus and rock.

Within a matter of hours night will fall, the dark sky will glitter with moon and stars, and sleep will force itself upon us. Life will continue on uninterrupted. Appreciated or not, the canvas of nature will go on being painted by the fingers of God.

In the midst of the offensive noise of our modern world—the people, the cars, the sounds, the smog, the heat, the pressures—there stand those reminders of his deep peace.

THE RUNNING WAVE, THE FLOWING AIR, THE QUIET EARTH, THE SHINING STARS, THE GENTLE NIGHT, THE HEALING LIGHT . . . AND FROM EACH, THE BLESSING OF THE DEEP PEACE OF CHRIST TO YOU, TO ME.

CHARLES SWINDOLL
THE FINISHING TOUCH

Jesus still had time for him. . .

DISCIPLINE IS EASY FOR ME TO SWALLOW. LOGICAL TO ASSIMILATE. MANAGEABLE AND APPROPRIATE.

But God's grace? Anything but.

Examples? How much time do you have?

David the psalmist becomes David the voyeur, but by God's grace becomes David the psalmist again.

Peter denied Christ before he preached Christ.

Zacchaeus, the crook. The cleanest part of his life was the money he'd laundered. But Jesus still had time for him. . . .

Story after story. Prayer after prayer. Surprise after surprise.

Seems that God is looking more for ways to get us home than for ways to keep us out. I challenge you to find one soul who came to God seeking grace and did not find it.

MAX LUCADO
WHEN GOD WHISPERS YOUR NAME

EW FEELINGS BRING A GREATER SENSE OF SATISFACTION THAN RELIEF, WHICH WEBSTER DEFINES AS "THE REMOVAL OR LIGHTENING OF SOMETHING OPPRESSIVE, PAINFUL, OR DISTRESSING." . . .

God calls this divine gift of relief *mercy*. That's right, *mercy*. It's a twin alongside *grace*.

Grace and mercy are usually seen together, but for some strange reason, mercy seems to live in grace's shadow, eclipsed by her popularity and prestige. . . .

If he were not rich in mercy, we might feel secure in God's love and we might be encouraged by his grace, but our lack of relief would hinder the presence of peace.

The essential link between God' s grace and our peace is his mercy . . . that is, God's infinite compassion actively demonstrated toward the miserable. Not just pity. Not simply sorrow or an understanding of our plight, but divine relief that results in peace deep within.

CHARLES SWINDOLL
THE FINISHING TOUCH

HOPE FOR TODAY *and* TOMORROW

ause and envision the scene in [God's] royal dining room. . . .

Driven not by our beauty but by his promise, he calls us to himself and invites us to take a permanent place at his table. Though we often limp more than we walk, we take our place next to the other sinners—made—saints and we share in God's glory.

May I share a partial list of what awaits you at his table?

You are beyond condemnation (Rom. 8:1).

You are delivered from the law (Rom. 7:6).

You are near God (Eph. 2:13).

You are a member of his kingdom (Col. 1: 13).

You have been adopted (Rom. 8:15).

You have access to God at any moment (Eph. 2:18).

You will never be abandoned (Heb. 13:5).

You have an imperishable inheritance (1 Pet. 1:4).

You possess (get this!) every spiritual blessing possible.

MAX LUCADO
IN THE GRIP OF GRACE

The story is told of a man who visited a stone quarry and asked three of the workers what they were doing.

"Can't you see?" said the first one irritably. "I'm cutting a stone!"

The second replied, "I'm earning a hundred pounds a week."

But the third put down his pick and thrust out his chest proudly. "I'm building a cathedral," he said.

People view work in many ways: as a necessary evil to keep bread on the table; as a means to a sizable bank account; as self-fulfillment and identity; as an economic obligation within society; as a means to a life of leisure.

Yet none of these represents an adequate view of work that provides ongoing or complete satisfaction for our labors. We are more than material beings, more than social beings, and more than cogs in the machinery of work.

We are, above all, spiritual beings, and as such we need to rediscover the moral and spiritual significance for every area and aspect of our lives, including our work.

Whether we are digging ditches, managing a bank, or cleaning houses, the important thing to remember is that we are building a cathedral.

CHARLES COLSON
WHY AMERICA DOESN'T WORK

omeone once counted all the promises in the Bible and came up with an amazing figure of almost 7500. Among that large number are some specific promises servants can claim today. Believe me, there are times when the only thing that will keep you going is a promise from God that your work is not in vain.

When we have done what was needed, but were ignored, misunderstood, or forgotten . . . we can be sure it was not in vain.

When we did what was right, with the right motive, but received no credit, no acknowledgment, not even a "thank you" . . . we have God's promise that "we shall reap."

When any servant has served and given and sacrificed and then willingly stepped aside for God to receive the glory, our heavenly Father promises he will receive back.

CHARLES SWINDOLL
THE FINISHING TOUCH

HE *WORD.* IN GREEK: *LOGOS.* It means knowledge, planning, design. That's how God created the world, and it's also how human beings create.

The crucial role of knowledge and design is perhaps best illustrated in computer technology. The silicon in a computer chip comes from ordinary sand. Yes, sand. What makes the chip so fantastically complex is the amount of human engineering and design that goes into it.

And consider the resources that are saved by computer technology. A fraction of an ounce of sand in a computer chip holds as much information as a library of books using tons of paper and ink. It performs the work once done by thousands of calculating machines made from tons of metal, using hundreds of reams of paper.

No, the doomsayers notwithstanding, we are not running out of resources.

We are just beginning to tap the greatest resource of all: the human mind, made in the image of God.

CHARLES COLSON
A DANCE WITH DECEPTION

JOY
in
LIVING

Seren-dip-ity—the *dip* of the *serene* into the common responsibilities of life. Serendipity occurs when something beautiful breaks into the monotonous and the mundane. A serendipitous life is marked by "surprisability" and spontaneity. When we lose our capacity for either, we settle into life's ruts. We expect little, and we're seldom disappointed.

Though I have walked with God for several decades, I must confess I still find much about him incomprehensible and mysterious. But this much I know: He delights in surprising us. He dots our pilgrimage from earth to heaven with amazing serendipities. . . .

Your situation may be as hot and barren as a desert or as forlorn and meaningless as a wasteland. You may be tempted to think, "There's no way!" when someone suggests things could change.

ALL I ASK IS THAT YOU . . . BE ON THE LOOKOUT. GOD MAY VERY WELL BE PLANNING A SERENDIPITY IN YOUR LIFE.

CHARLES SWINDOLL
THE FINISHING TOUCH

ATURING FAITH—FAITH THAT DEEPENS AND GROWS AS WE LIVE OUR CHRISTIAN LIFE—IS NOT JUST KNOWLEDGE, BUT KNOWLEDGE ACTED UPON. It is not just belief, but belief lived out—practiced. James said we are to be doers of the Word, not just hearers.

Dietrick Bonhoeffer, the German pastor martyred in a Nazi concentration camp, succinctly stated this crucial interrelationship: "Only he who believes is obedient; only he who is obedient believes." . . .

Like learning to balance a bicycle or mastering a foreign language, faith is a state of mind that grows out of our actions, just as it also governs them. Obedience is the key to real faith.

CHARLES COLSON
LOVING GOD

Let's serve . . . in the name of Jesus.

SERVANTHOOD IMPLIES DILIGENCE, FAITHFULNESS, LOYALTY, AND HUMILITY.

Servants don't compete . . . or grandstand . . . or polish their image . . . or grab the limelight. They know their job, they admit their limitations, they do what they do quietly and consistently.

Servants cannot control anyone or everything, and they shouldn't try.

Servants cannot change or "fix" people.

Servants cannot explain many of the great things that happen.

Servants cannot meet most folks' expectations.

Servants cannot concern themselves with who gets the credit. . . .

Let's serve . . . in the name of Jesus.

CHARLES SWINDOLL
THE FINISHING TOUCH

ant to see a miracle? Plant a word of love heartdeep in a person's life. Nurture it with a smile and a prayer, and watch what happens.

An employee gets a compliment. A wife receives a bouquet of flowers. A cake is baked and carried next door. A widow is hugged. A gas-station attendant is honored. A preacher is praised.

Sowing seeds of peace is like sowing beans. You don't know why it works; you just know it does. Seeds are planted, and topsoils of hurt are shoved away.

DON'T FORGET THE PRINCIPLE. NEVER UNDERESTIMATE THE POWER OF A SEED.

MAX LUCADO
THE APPLAUSE OF HEAVEN

HEN JOYCE PAGE ARRIVES AT THE PRISON GATE EACH WEEKDAY AT NOON, THE GUARDS WAVE HER THROUGH. Prison officials ask how her kids are doing. After all, Joyce has been spending her lunch hour at the St. Louis County Correctional Institution just about every weekday since 1979.

Joyce began going to the prison with her supervisor, also a Christian. When the supervisor was transferred, Joyce continued by herself, leaving her office carrying a peanut butter sandwich while other secretaries bustled off in clusters for the cafeteria.

Each day Joyce meets with a different group of inmates, from the men in isolation to a small group of women prisoners. "Sometimes we have a worship service," she says, "or a time of testimony and singing, or in-depth Bible study and discussion."

When Joyce slips back to her desk at one o'clock, one of her co-workers is usually already bemoaning her lunchtime excesses and loudly proclaiming that she really will have the diet plate tomorrow. Joyce laughs to herself. She knows exactly what she'll have for lunch tomorrow—another peanut butter sandwich at the wheel of her car on the way to prison. . . .

Holiness is obeying God—sharing his love, even when it is inconvenient.

CHARLES COLSON
LOVING GOD

With each new dawn,

life delivers a package to

your front door, rings

your doorbell, and runs.

Charles Swindoll

ALIVE AND GROWING!

PERSEVERING
THROUGH
GOOD TIMES
and
BAD

AKE FROM US OUR WEALTH AND WE ARE HINDERED. TAKE OUR HEALTH AND WE ARE HANDICAPPED. TAKE OUR PURPOSE AND WE ARE SLOWED, TEMPORARILY CONFUSED. But take away our hope, and we are plunged into deepest darkness . . . stopped dead in our tracks, paralyzed. Wondering, "Why?" Asking, "How much longer? Will this darkness ever end? Does he know where I am?"

Then the Father says, "That's far enough," and how sweet it is! Like blossoms in the snow, long–awaited color returns to our life. The stream, once frozen, starts to thaw. Hope revives and washes over us.

Inevitably, spring follows winter. Every year. Yes, including this one. Barren days, like naked limbs, will soon be clothed with fresh life. Do you need that reminder today? Are you ready for some sunshine on your shoulders . . . a few green sprouts poking up through all that white? A light at the end of your tunnel?

Look! There it is in the distance. It may be tiny, but it's there.

CHARLES SWINDOLL
THE FINISHING TOUCH

Rest on this earth is a false rest. Beware of those who urge you to find happiness here; you won't find it. Guard against the false physicians who promise that joy is only a diet away, a marriage away, a job away, or a transfer away. . . .

Try this. Imagine a perfect world. Whatever that means to you, imagine it. Does that mean peace? Then envision absolute tranquility. Does a perfect world imply joy? Then create your highest happiness. Will a perfect world have love? If so, ponder a place where love has no bounds. Whatever heaven means to you, imagine it. Get it firmly fixed in your mind. Delight in it. Dream about it. Long for it.

And then smile as the Father reminds you, *No one has ever imagined what God has prepared for those who love him.* . . .

WHEN IT COMES TO DESCRIBING HEAVEN, WE ARE ALL HAPPY FAILURES.

MAX LUCADO
WHEN GOD WHISPERS YOUR NAME

What does it mean to have a biblically trained mind? Many Christians think of biblical faith in very narrow terms. We think of it as religion—as something expressed in church attendance, prayer, and worship—without much relevance to the larger world outside.

But that's not the biblical view. The biblical view is that faith has to do with all of life. Every decision we make reflects what we believe and what we value.

A vivid example can be seen in the life of Abraham Kuyper, a great Dutch theologian in the early part of this century. Kuyper argued that to stand against a comprehensive secularism, we must articulate a Christian philosophy that is equally comprehensive. We must see Christianity as an all embracing system of thought that gives us a perspective from which to view every part of life: family, church, work, politics, science, art, and culture.

IN SHORT, CHRISTIANITY MUST BE A WORLD-VIEW: A VIEW OF THE ENTIRE WORLD, AN INTELLECTUAL GRID THROUGH WHICH WE CAN INTERPRET EVERYTHING WE SEE OR READ OR DO. GOD CREATED THE WORLD, AND EVERYTHING IN THE WORLD RELATES IN SOME WAY TO HIM.

CHARLES COLSON
A DANCE WITH DECEPTION

here did Christians get the idea that we'd be appreciated, affirmed, and admired? The Savior himself taught that blessings are reserved for the persecuted, for those who are reviled, for those against whom folks say all kinds of evil . . . falsely . . . (Matt. 5:10–11). . . .

It sure is easy to forget those words and get soft, becoming too tender, too sensitive. Fragility is not a virtue extolled in Scripture. Saints with thin skin get distracted and, shortly thereafter, discouraged. There is a long, demanding course to be run, most of which takes place in the trenches and without applause. I suggest we lower our expectations as we intensify our determination and head for the goal.

ENDURANCE IS THE SECRET, NOT POPULARITY.

CHARLES SWINDOLL
THE FINISHING TOUCH

ECAUSE IT IS SHORT, LIFE IS PACKED WITH CHALLENGING POSSIBILITIES. Because it is uncertain, it's filled with challenging adjustments. I'm convinced that's much of what Jesus meant when he promised us an abundant life. Abundant with challenges, running over with possibilities, filled with opportunities to adapt, shift, alter, and change. Come to think of it, that's the secret of staying young. It is also the path that leads to optimism and motivation.

With each new dawn, life delivers a package to your front door, rings your doorbell, and runs. Each package is cleverly wrapped in paper with big print. One package reads: "Watch out. Better worry about this!" Another: "Danger. This will bring fear!" And another: "Impossible. You'll never handle this one!"

When you hear that ring tomorrow morning, try something new. Have Jesus Christ answer the door for you.

CHARLES SWINDOLL
THE FINISHING TOUCH

GOD'S
Power:
OUR
Potential

 HE ILLUSIONS OF OUR CULTURE HAVE US BELIEVING THAT ONLY BIG NAMES OR BIG ORGANIZATIONS CAN ACCOMPLISH ANYTHING. And so we send our checks off to worldwide Christian ministries and settle back in the easy chair. We serve God by remote control.

In truth, the most important work of the gospel is done directly by citizens living out their biblical responsibility in their everyday circumstances. This is one reason I look forward to visiting Third World countries. In most there are no evangelical superstars, no big organizations, and so those "poor" Christians simply go out and obey the gospel themselves.

In Madagascar, I found that the diligent efforts of one man kept alive several hundred inmates. I was so moved I asked if there was anything I could do to help, expecting him to say, "send money." "Oh, no," came his astonishing reply, "our God is sufficient for all things."

CHARLES COLSON
CHRISTIANITY TODAY, FEBRUARY 5, 1990

e admire pioneers . . . so long as we can just read about them, not finance their journeys. We applaud explorers . . . but not if it means we have to load up and travel with them. Creative ideas are fine . . . "but don't get carried away," we warn. . . .

When it came time for God to send his Son to earth, he did not send him to the palace of some mighty king. He was conceived in the womb of an unwed mother—a virgin!—who lived in the lowly village of Nazareth.

In choosing those who would represent Christ and establish his church, God picked some of the most unusual individuals imaginable: unschooled fishermen, a tax collector(!), a mystic, a doubter, and a former Pharisee who had persecuted Christians. He continued to pick some very unusual persons down through the ages. In fact, he seems to delight in such surprising choices to this very day.

SO, LET GOD BE GOD.
EXPECT THE UNEXPECTED.

CHARLES SWINDOLL
THE FINISHING TOUCH

Though you hear nothing, he is speaking.

WHY DOES GOD WAIT UNTIL THE MONEY IS GONE? WHY DOES HE WAIT UNTIL THE SICKNESS HAS LINGERED? WHY DOES HE CHOOSE TO WAIT UNTIL THE OTHER SIDE OF THE GRAVE TO ANSWER THE PRAYERS FOR HEALING?

I don't know. I only know his timing is always right. I can only say he will do what is best. "God will always give what is right to his people who cry to him night and day, and he will not be slow to answer them" (Luke 18:7).

Though you hear nothing, he is speaking. Though you see nothing, he is acting. With God there are no accidents. Every incident is intended to bring us closer to him.

MAX LUCADO
A GENTLE THUNDER

hrist gave the church a commission: the Great Commission. It was a call to make disciples—to baptize men and women and teach them to observe all that Christ commanded. To equip the saints, as Paul's letter to the Ephesians says.

The process of being equipped is like military training. I can't help but remember my own experience in the Marines. Intense physical training. Death-defying obstacle courses. Nerve-racking field exercises. . . .

Shouldn't it be the same for the soldiers of the cross? . . .

If you're looking for a church, find one that realizes that it is the basic school of discipline and training for Christians. Pick a church where you will be best equipped for the spiritual battle raging around us. . . . It's a battle for eternal souls. And no Christian can afford to be just a weekend warrior.

CHARLES COLSON
A DANGEROUS GRACE

GROWING UP
in
CHRIST

When it comes to irritations, I've found that it helps if I remember that I am not in charge of my day . . . God is. And while I'm sure he wants me to use my time wisely, he is more concerned with the development of my character and the cultivation of the qualities that make me Christlike within. One of his preferred methods of training is through adjustments to irritations.

A perfect illustration? The oyster and its pearl.

Pearls are the products of irritation. This irritation occurs when the shell of the oyster is invaded by an alien substance like a grain of sand. When that happens, all the resources within the tiny, sensitive oyster rush to the irritated spot and begin to release healing fluids that otherwise would have remained dormant. By and by the irritant is covered—by a pearl. Had there been no irritating interruption, there could have been no pearl.

NO WONDER OUR HEAVENLY HOME HAS PEARLY GATES TO WELCOME THE WOUNDED AND BRUISED WHO HAVE RESPONDED CORRECTLY TO THE STING OF IRRITATIONS.

CHARLES SWINDOLL
THE FINISHING TOUCH

ANY CHRISTIANS ASSOCIATE HOLINESS WITH A LONG STRING OF "DO'S AND DON'TS." BUT SEEING HOLINESS ONLY AS RULE-KEEPING BREEDS SERIOUS PROBLEMS.

First, it limits the scope of true biblical holiness, which must affect every aspect of our lives.

Second, even though the rules may be biblically based, we often end up obeying the rules rather than obeying God; concern with the letter of the law can cause us to lose its spirit.

Third, emphasis on rule-keeping deludes us into thinking we can be holy through our efforts. But there can be no holiness apart from the work of the Holy Spirit—in quickening us through the conviction of sin and bringing us by grace to Christ, and in sanctifying us—for it is grace that causes us even to want to be holy.

And finally, our pious efforts can become ego-gratifying, as if holy living were some kind of spiritual beauty contest. Such self-centered spirituality in turn leads to self-righteousness— the very opposite of the selflessness of true holiness.

CHARLES COLSON
LOVING GOD

Jesus will wash . . . the grimiest part of your life.

TO PLACE OUR FEET IN THE BASIN OF JESUS IS TO PLACE THE FILTHIEST PARTS OF OUR LIVES INTO HIS HANDS. IN THE ANCIENT EAST, PEOPLE'S FEET WERE CAKED WITH MUD AND DIRT. The servant of the feast saw to it that the feet were cleaned. Jesus is assuming the role of the servant. He will wash the grimiest part of your life.

If you let him. The water of the Servant comes only when we confess that we are dirty. Only when we confess that we are caked with filth, that we have walked forbidden trails and followed the wrong paths. . . .

We will never be cleansed until we confess we are dirty. We will never be pure until we admit we are filthy. And we will never be able to wash the feet of those who have hurt us until we allow Jesus, the one we have hurt, to wash ours.

MAX LUCADO
A GENTLE THUNDER

esus Christ turned conventional views of power upside down. When his disciples argued over who was the greatest, Jesus rebuked them. "The greatest among you should be like the youngest, and the one who rules like the one who serves," he said. Imagine the impact his statement would make in the back rooms of American politicians or in the carpeted boardrooms of big business—or, sadly, in some religious councils.

Jesus was as good as his words. He washed his own followers' dusty feet, a chore reserved for the lowliest servant of first-century Palestine. A king serving the mundane physical needs of his subjects? Incomprehensible. Yet servant leadership is the heart of Christ's teaching, "Whoever wants to be first must be slave of all."

CHARLES COLSON
KINGDOMS IN CONFLICT

"God has planted eternity

in the hearts of men."

Ecclesiastes 3:10 TLB

VICTORIOUS, TODAY AND TOMORROW

POWER
Through
PRAYER

It occurred to me last week that there is a practical reason Thanksgiving always precedes Christmas: It sets in motion the ideal mental attitude to carry us through the weeks in between. In other words, a sustained spirit of gratitude makes the weeks before Christmas a celebration rather than a marathon.

Maybe these few thoughts will stimulate you to give God your own thanks in greater abundance.

. . . thank You Lord:

for Your sovereign control over our circumstances
for Your holy character in spite of our sinfulness
for Your commitment to us even when we wander astray
for Your Word that gives us direction
for Your love that holds us close
for Your gentle compassion in our sorrows
for Your consistent faithfulness through our highs and lows . . .
for Your understanding when we are confused
for Your Spirit that enlightens our eyes
for Your grace that removes our guilt

CHARLES SWINDOLL
THE FINISHING TOUCH

o you want to know how to deepen your prayer life? Pray. Don't prepare to pray. Just pray. Don't read about prayer. Just pray. Don't attend a lecture on prayer or engage in discussion about prayer. Just pray.

Posture, tone, and place are personal matters. Select the form that works for you. But don't think about it too much. Don't be so concerned about wrapping the gift that you never give it. Better to pray awkwardly than not at all.

AND IF YOU FEEL YOU SHOULD ONLY PRAY WHEN INSPIRED, THAT'S OKAY. JUST SEE TO IT THAT YOU ARE INSPIRED EVERY DAY.

MAX LUCADO
WHEN GOD WHISPERS YOUR NAME

ow it is important to remember that some of the most profound ministries of the Spirit of God are not public or loud or large. Sometimes his most meaningful touch on our lives comes when we are all alone.

I urge you to include in your schedule time to be alone with God. I am fortunate to live within ninety minutes of the mountains . . . and less than forty-five minutes from the beach. Those are great places to commune with God. You do have places where you can get away for a long walk, don't you? I hope it's in a wooded area. The gentle breeze blowing through the forest is therapeutic. Sometimes just being alone out in God's marvelous creation is all that's needed for the scales to be removed from your eyes and for you to silence the harassment and the noise of your day and begin to hear from God.

CHARLES SWINDOLL
FLYING CLOSER TO THE FLAME

HE SCRIPTURES ARE REPLETE WITH REFERENCES TO THE VALUE OF WAITING FOR THE LORD AND SPENDING TIME WITH HIM. When we do, the debris we have gathered during the hurried, busy hours of our day gets filtered out, not unlike the silt that settles where a river widens. With the debris out of the way, we are able to see things more clearly and feel God's nudgings more sensitively.

David frequently underscored the benefits of solitude. I am certain he first became acquainted with this discipline as he kept his father's sheep. Later, during those tumultuous years when King Saul was borderline insane and pursuing him out of jealousy, David found his time with God not only a needed refuge but his means of survival. . . .

GOD STILL LONGS TO SPEAK TO WAITING HEARTS . . . HEARTS THAT ARE QUIET BEFORE HIM.

CHARLES SWINDOLL
THE FINISHING TOUCH

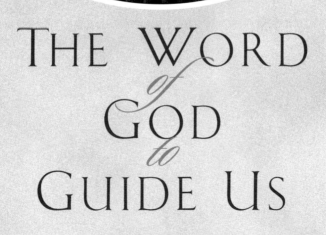

THE WORD

of

GOD

to

GUIDE US

he Bible—banned, burned, beloved. More widely read, more frequently attacked than any other book in history. Generations of intellectuals have attempted to discredit it; dictators of every age have outlawed it and executed those who read it.

Yet fragments of the Bible smuggled into solitary prison cells have transformed ruthless killers into gentle saints. Pieced—together scraps of Scripture have converted whole villages of Indians.

Yearly, the Bible outsells every best—seller. Portions have been translated into more than eighteen hundred languages and even carried to the moon. . . .

The Bible's power rests upon the fact that it is the reliable, errorless, and infallible Word of God.

CHARLES COLSON
LOVING GOD

here is something grand about old things that are still in good shape. Old furniture, rich with the patina of age and history, is far more intriguing than the uncomfortable, modern stuff. When you sit on it or eat off it or sleep in it, your mind pictures those in previous centuries who did the same in a world of candlelight, oil lamps, buggies, outhouses, and potbelly stoves. Each scrape or dent holds a story you wish you knew. . . .

The Bible is old also—ancient, in fact. Its timeless stories have for centuries shouted, "You can make it! Don't quit . . . don t give up!" Its truths, secure and solid as stone, say, "I'm still here, waiting to be claimed and applied." Whether it's a prophet's warning, a patriarch's prayer, a poet's psalm, or a preacher's challenging reminder. The Book of books lives on, offering us new vistas. . . .

Though ancient, it has never lost its relevance. Though battered, no one has ever improved on its content. Though old, it never fails to offer something pure, something wise, something new.

CHARLES SWINDOLL
THE FINISHING TOUCH

In 1993, archaeologists digging in the Near East made a remarkable discovery about King David. They uncovered a rock fragment inscribed with an ancient text referring to "the House of David," a phrase used for the ruling dynasty founded by King David. The rock appears to be a victory monument erected by a Syrian king nearly three thousand years after a battle described in 1 Kings.

What makes the finding so significant is that it's the first reference to King David or his royal family found outside the pages of the Bible—providing new external evidence for the historical reliability of the Bible.

This is by no means the first time archaeology has supported the Bible. Time and time again, critics have flatly stated that some portion of the Bible could not be true. Time and time again, archaeologists chipping away with their hammers have uncovered stunning support for the biblical text. . . .

From the late nineteenth century, when archaeology first became a science, the Bible has been proved reliable on all levels—religious *and* historical.

THE GOD OF FAITH IS ALSO THE GOD OF HISTORY.

CHARLES COLSON
A DANGEROUS GRACE

FRIENDS *and* FAMILY: THE BODY *of* CHRIST

You guessed it. We need each other.

NOBODY IS A WHOLE CHAIN. Each one is a link. But take away one link and the chain is broken.

Nobody is a whole team. Each one is a player. But take away one player and the game is forfeited.

Nobody is a whole orchestra. Each one is a musician. But take away one musician and the symphony is incomplete. . . .

You guessed it. We need each other. You need someone and someone needs you. Isolated islands we're not.

To make this thing called life work, we gotta lean and support. And relate and respond. And give and take. And confess and forgive. And reach out and embrace. And release and rely. . . .

Since none of us is a whole, independent, self-sufficient, superb-capable, all-powerful hotshot, let's quit acting like we are. Life's lonely enough without our playing that silly role

The game's over. Let's link up.

CHARLES SWINDOLL
THE FINISHING TOUCH

130

FTER THE ROMAN EMPIRE FELL,
CHAOS RULED EUROPE.

Warring bands of illiterate Germanic
tribes opposed and deposed one another.
People were scattered across the land in crude huts and rough
towns. Early medieval Europe seemed destined for complete
barbarism.

One force prevented this. The church.

Instead of conforming to the barbarian culture of the
Dark Ages, the medieval church modeled a counterculture to
a world engulfed by destruction and confusion. Thousands of
monastic orders spread across Europe, characterized by
discipline, creativity, and a moral order lacking in the world
around them. . . .

Like the monastic communities of the Middle Ages, the
church today can serve as outposts of truth, decency, and
civilization in the darkening culture around us.

CHARLES COLSON
AGAINST THE NIGHT

ave you ever noticed how uniquely adapted each animal is to its environment and its way of life? On land, a duck waddles along ungainly on its webbed feet. In the water, it glides along smooth as glass. The rabbit runs with ease and great bursts of speed, but I've never seen one swimming laps. The squirrel climbs anything in sight but cannot fly (unless you count great airborne leaps from limb to limb), while the eagle soars to mountaintops.

Each creature has its own set of capabilities with which it will naturally excel . . .

God has placed you in his family and given you a certain mixture that makes you unique. No mixture is insignificant!

That mix pleases him completely. Nobody else is exactly like you. That should bring you pleasure, too.

When you operate in your realm of capabilities, you will excel and the whole Body will benefit . . . and you will experience incredible satisfaction.

CHARLES SWINDOLL
THE FINISHING TOUCH

What we do flows from who we are. . . .

THE CHURCH'S ROLE IN THE WORLD IS NOT A SERIES OF INDEPENDENT ITEMS ON AN ACTION CHECKLIST. INSTEAD, THE CHURCH'S ROLE (WHAT IT DOES) IS DEPENDENT ON ITS CHARACTER (WHAT IT IS) AS A COMMUNITY OF BELIEVERS.

What we do flows from who we are. . . .

If the church is the Body, the holy presence of Christ in the world, its most fundamental task is to build communities of holy character. And the first priority of those communities is to disciple men and women to maturity in Christ and then equip them to live their faith in every aspect of life and in every part of the world.

CHARLES COLSON
THE BODY

133

HEAVEN,
Sweet Home

Our heart song won't be silenced until we see the dawn.

THERE DWELLS INSIDE YOU, DEEP WITHIN, A TINY WHIPPOORWILL. LISTEN. YOU WILL HEAR HIM SING. HIS ARIA MOURNS THE DUSK. HIS SOLO SIGNALS THE DAWN.

It is the song of the whippoorwill.

He will not be silent until the sun is seen.

We forget he is there, so easy is he to ignore. Other animals of the heart are larger, noisier, more demanding, more imposing.

But none is so constant.

Other creatures of the soul are more quickly fed. More simply satisfied. We feed the lion who growls for power. We stroke the tiger who demands affection. We bridle the stallion who bucks control.

(CONTINUED)

135

But what do we do with the whippoorwill who yearns for eternity?

For that is his song. That is his task. Out of the gray he sings a golden song. Perched in time he chirps a timeless verse. Peering through pain's shroud, he sees a painless place. Of that place he sings.

And though we try to ignore him, we cannot. He is us, and his song is ours. Our heart song won't be silenced until we see the dawn.

"God has planted eternity in the hearts of men" (Eccles. 3:10 TLB), says the wise man. But it doesn't take a wise person to know that people long for more than earth. When we see pain, we yearn. When we see hunger, we question why. Senseless deaths. Endless tears, needless loss. Where do they come from? Where will they lead?

(CONTINUED)

Isn't there more to life than death?

And so sings the whippoorwill.

Unhappiness on earth cultivates a hunger for heaven. By gracing us with a deep dissatisfaction, God holds our attention. The only tragedy, then, is to be satisfied prematurely. To settle for earth. To be content in a strange land. To intermarry with the Babylonians and forget Jerusalem.

We are not happy here because we are not at home here. We are not happy here because we are not supposed to be happy here. We are "like foreigners and strangers in this world" (1 Pet. 2:11). . . .

And you will never be completely happy on earth simply because you were not made for earth. Oh, you will have your moments of joy. You will catch glimpses of light. You will know moments or even days of peace. But they simply do not compare with the happiness that lies ahead.

MAX LUCADO
WHEN GOD WHISPERS YOUR NAME

One of the great doctrines of Christianity is our belief in a heavenly home. Ultimately, we shall spend eternity with God in the place he has prepared for us. And part of that exciting anticipation is his promise to reward his servants for a job well done. Scripture not only supports the idea of eternal rewards, it spells out the specifics. . . .

Most rewards are received in heaven, not on earth. Now don't misunderstand. There are earthly rewards. But when it comes to servanthood, God reserves special honor for that day when "each man's work will become evident" and "he shall receive a reward" (3: 13-14).

All rewards are based on quality, not quantity. We humans are impressed with size and volume and noise and numbers. It is easy to forget that God's eye is always on motive. . . .

No reward that is postponed will be forgotten. God doesn't settle his accounts at the end of every day. Nor does he close out his books toward the end of everyone's life. But when that day in eternity dawns, when time shall be no more on this earth, no act of serving others—be it well-known or unknown to others—will be forgotten. . . .

CHARLES SWINDOLL
THE FINISHING TOUCH

 HE BOOK OF REVELATION COULD BE ENTITLED *THE BOOK OF HOMECOMING,* FOR IN IT WE ARE GIVEN A PICTURE OF OUR HEAVENLY HOME.

John's descriptions of the future steal your breath. His depiction of the final battle is graphic. Good clashes with evil. The sacred encounters the sinful. The pages howl with the shrieks of dragons and smolder with the coals of fiery pits. But in the midst of the battlefield there is a rose. John describes it in chapter 21:

Then I saw a new heaven and a new earth, for the first heaven and the first earth had passed away, and there was no longer any sea. I saw the Holy City, the new Jerusalem, coming down out of heaven from God, prepared as a bride beautifully dressed for her husband. . . .

In this final mountaintop encounter, God pulls back the curtain and allows the warrior to peek into the homeland. When given the task of writing down what he sees, John chooses the most beautiful comparison earth has to offer. The Holy City, John says, is like "a bride beautifully dressed for her husband."

MAX LUCADO
THE APPLAUSE OF HEAVEN

Our
Hearts Are
at
Rest

Contentment is something we must learn. It isn't a trait we're born with. But the question is *how?* In 1 Timothy 6 we find a couple of very practical answers to that question:

A current perspective on eternity: "For we have brought nothing into the world, so we cannot take anything out of it either" (v. 7).

A simple acceptance of essentials: "And if we have food and covering, with these we shall be content" (v. 8).

Both attitudes work beautifully. . . .

You see, society's plan of attack is to create dissatisfaction, to convince us that we must be in a constant pursuit for something "out there" that is sure to bring us happiness. When you reduce that lie to its lowest level, it is saying that contentment is impossible without striving for more.

God's Word offers the exact opposite advice: Contentment is possible when we stop striving for more. Contentment never comes from externals. Never!

As a Greek sage once put it: "To whom little is not enough, nothing is enough."

CHARLES SWINDOLL
THE FINISHING TOUCH

here are many rooms in my father's house."

What a tender phrase. A house implies rest, safety, warmth, a table, a bed, a place to be at home. But this isn't just any house. It is our Father's house.

All of us know what it is like to be in a house that is not our own. Perhaps you've spent time in a dorm room or army barrack. Maybe you've slept in your share of hotels or bunked in a few hostels. They have beds. They have tables. They may have food and they may be warm, but they are a far cry from being "your father's house."

Your father's house is where your father is. . . .

We don't always feel welcome here on earth. We wonder if there is a place here for us. People can make us feel unwanted. Tragedy leaves us feeling like intruders. Strangers. Interlopers in a land not ours. We don't always feel welcome here.

We shouldn't. This isn't our home. To feel unwelcome is no tragedy. Indeed it is healthy. We are not home here. This language we speak, it's not ours. This body we wear, it isn't us. And the world we live in, this isn't home.

MAX LUCADO
A GENTLE THUNDER

. . . *to witness the Savior, you have to get on your knees.*

A SMALL CATHEDRAL OUTSIDE BETHLEHEM MARKS THE SUPPOSED BIRTHPLACE OF JESUS. Behind a high altar in the church is a cave, a little cavern lit by silver lamps.

You can enter the main edifice and admire the ancient church. You can also enter the quiet cave where a star embedded in the floor recognizes the birth of the King. There is one stipulation, however. You have to stoop. The door is so low you can't go in standing up.

The same is true of the Christ. You can see the world standing tall, but to witness the Savior, you have to get on your knees.

MAX LUCADO
THE APPLAUSE OF HEAVEN

Acknowledgments

Grateful acknowledgment is made to the following publishers and copyright holders for permission to reprint copyrighted material:

CHARLES COLSON

- *Life Sentence.* Tarrytown, NY: Fleming H. Revell. © Charles Colson/Fleming H. Revell, 1979.
- *Loving God.* Grand Rapids: Zondervan. © Charles Colson/Zondervan, 1983.
- *Who Speaks for God?* Westchester, Ill. Crossway Books. © Fellowship Communications, 1985.
- *Kingdoms in Conflict.* Grand Rapids: Zondervan, © Charles Colson/William Morrow, 1987.
- *Against the Night.* Ann Arbor: Servant. © Fellowship Communications, 1989.
- *Christianity Today,* February 5, 1990. © Charles Colson, 1990.
- *Why America Doesn't Work.* Dallas: Word. © Charles Colson, 1991.
- *The Body.* Dallas: Word. © Charles Colson, 1992.
- "Enduring Revolution." Templeton Address. © Charles Colson, 1993.

- *A Dance with Deception.* Dallas: Word. © Prison Fellowship, 1995.
- *A Dangerous Grace.* Dallas: Word. © Prison Fellowship, 1994.

MAX LUCADO

- *The Applause of Heaven.* Dallas: Word. © Max Lucado, 1990, 1996.
- *When God Whispers Your Name.* Dallas: Word. © Max Lucado, 1994.
- *A Gentle Thunder.* Dallas: Word. © Max Lucado, 1995.
- *In the Grip of Grace.* Dallas: Word. © Max Lucado, 1996.

CHARLES SWINDOLL

- *The Grace Awakening.* Dallas: Word. © Charles Swindoll, 1990.
- *The Finishing Touch.* Dallas: Word. © Charles Swindoll, 1994.
- *Flying Closer to the Flame.* Dallas: Word. © Charles Swindoll, 1993, 1995